FOR
INSPIRATION, FAITH, TRUTH AND HEALING

Where We Are Now Series.
VOLUME 2

Sharon Cully

WHERE WE ARE NOW

Copyright © 2014 Sharon Cully

The moral right of Sharon Cully to be identified as the Author of the work and Emma Jarvis as the Artist has been asserted by them in accordance with the Copyright, Designs and Patents Act 1988. All rights reserved. No part of this book may be used or reproduced by any means, graphic, electronic, or mechanical, including photocopying, recording, taping or by any information storage retrieval system without the written permission of the publisher except in the case of brief quotations embodied in critical articles and reviews.

National Library of Australia Cataloguing-in-Publication entry
Author: Cully, Sharon, author.
Title: Poetry for Inspiration, Faith, Truth and Healing / Sharon Cully ; Emma Jarvis, artist.
ISBN: 9780992365349 (paperback)
Series: Where We are Now – Past and Future; Volume 2.
Other Authors/Contributors: Jarvis, Emma, artist.
Dewey Number: A821.4

Publishing Details
Published in Australia

Printed & Channel Distribution in US/UK/AUS / Canada
Printed through Lightning Source (USA/UK/AUS)
Available via:

Printed & Channel Distribution in US/UK/Canada/Aus
Lightning Source (USA/UK/AUS)
Available via:
United States - Ingram Book Company; Amazon.com; Baker & Taylor and others
Canada - Chapters Indigo; Amazon Canada and others
United Kingdom - Amazon.com; Bertrams; Book Depository Ltd; Gardners; Mallory International and others
Australia - DA Information Services; The Nile; Emporium Books Online; James Bennet (Australian Libraries) Dennis Jones and Associates; and others

For further exploration any of the material contained within this book the following contact details have been provided:

Written By:	Sharon Cully. Where We are Now – Past and Future
Web Site:	www.wherewearenow.com.au
Email:	sharon@wherewearenow.com.au
Illustrated by:	Emma Jarvis. Multidimensional Energy Patterns
Web Site:	www.energypatterns.net
Email:	mdenergypatterns@gmail.com

TABLE OF CONTENTS

Preface iv
Acknowledgements vi
To Simply Be 2
Truth 4
Reality 6
Illusion 8
Free Fall 10
Loss Of Innocence 12
Understanding Evolves 14
In Spirit 16
Limitations 18
The Divine 20
Ever Present 22
Dawn Of Awareness 24
I Stumble 26
Emotions And Feelings 28
Touch 30
The Gentle Touch 32
Uplifted 34
Sharon Cully - Author 36
Emma Jarvis - Artist 39

Preface

My life has been a rich one with a roller-coaster of emotions. I have been a Registered Nurse for forty years. Nursing combined with my personal experiences has helped me form a deep understanding about the journey we are all on. I have been on my knees more times than I care to remember. In the end it was discovering the saving power, grace and love of God that helped me rise. Rise beyond the turmoil and trauma that this life put before me. So I found that quite without meaning to I have been working on an experiential "How to survive" manual. I developed skills the hard way. These skills have enabled me to provide an ongoing, deep and satisfying service to others from all walks of life.

Along this journey I discovered the gift for expressing these emotions through the written word. These words now come as poetry and hold the key to overcoming. This collection of poems came from the very heart of me. With the love of God, together we have been any to lay them here for others who may find themselves in need of comfort. Each poem has its own unique illustrated pattern providing the reader with maximum benefit along with these words. The patterns depict the words of each poem demonstrated in energy form. These have been provided by my daughter who also shares her gifts given from God for the benefit of others. Please join me on this, the second volume in the Where We Are Now Series. I invite you to come with me on the next stage of the journey home.

Acknowledgements

No collection of words is complete without the acknowledgement of those who have supported the process. Thanks must go to my family who have supported and loved me throughout all these times in my life. They always help me climb up the ladder again.

My husband Peter has often been left to cope with finishing of the evening meal as I am apt to disappear for hours as a new idea arrived.

My mother Eileen who passed on her gift of writing and poetry to me.

My father Bert who listened for hours to all my strange musings.

My daughter Emma proof reader extraordinaire. I thank you for the gift of your illustrated multidimensional energy patterns that provide additional comfort on many levels to those who read these poems.

My children Peter and Michael for putting up with my eccentricities

and loving me anyway.

For all the people who have coloured my tapestry of life I thank you.

Above all I give my thanks to God, who has been there at every moment to herald my strengths and to supply Grace to my failings..

.

To Simply Be

To see all previous beliefs fall under the hammer;
to realise that in the wider picture belief doesn't matter.
Rules and hypothesis that once caused me to falter;
in the end are simply a second in time, a stutter.

The world is what we make it;
it is how we let the pieces fit.
Man made the parameters and the split;
all things really should be allowed to simply be and sit.

Truth

When what I thought was Truth was not;
my Faith in things began to fall.
When I realised what I saw with my eyes wasn't it all;
it was time to rethink Life and what is not life at all.

Reality

The walls of my reality shatter and fall;
reality is something different to one and all.
Reality can be fleeting but real;
leaving us to look in wonder to sense and feel.

Illusion

Things are not what they seem.
They at times are seen as though a dream.
Sometimes they overlap or blur.
Sometimes a time lapse is given a gentle stir.

Edges do not always line up as if by sewing.
Shadows linger and at times come to overflowing.
Colour can fade or waver in and out.
Or it can be crisp, clean and deliver a clout.

Is that tree really a tree?
Is that sense of free really free?
Is that border really the edge of a sea?
Or is that edge simply another part of me?

Is up, up or is it down?
Is it down or from other places renown?
Is in really in, or is it out?
Or is it simply just spreading itself all about?

Is it over lapsing or overlaying?
Is it simply spreading and staying?
Is past present and future simply outlaying?
Or is it really the "I Am" saying?

What is what?
Which is "which" and which is "what"?
Which "which" really is and which "which" is not?
Is it really just some devious game and mind plot?

Relax and just let it be.
Let it all flow, mix, mingle and be free.
No rules, no laws instead an endless sea.
Everything is simply swirling around me.

When you relax, breathe and be.
Open your eyes to all possibility.
All realities bared for you to see.
That One is All, All is One and All is simply me.

Free Fall

When you don't see what you think you see.
When what I think is you is a reflection of me.
When you don't hear what you think you hear.
When the front is out there or at my rear.

When you feel presence in an empty room.
When you see inside your cupboard not simply a broom.
When you feel all your hairs standing in the air.
When everything in you seems to make your body stop and stare.

Reach out, hold on don't slide.
God will be there to direct and guide.
Faith finds you resting, safe in a cocoon of lace.
Belief in the higher good will be your saving grace.

When the void feels full.
You stand still in time and mull.
Never lonely, feeling all the others.
At times though, the feeling wraps and smothers.

With a sense of love.
A smooth feel like a glove.
The surroundings remain welcoming and free.
The Light revealing and sharing all with me.

The knowledge that all is one.
That Life as we know it is not dusted and done.
Instead I feel whole with a sense of belonging.
This presence fulfils my longing.

Loss Of Innocence

One by one each fact I thought right is not.
One by one beliefs and truths become not.
Truth revealed has become change.
My understanding finally has free range.

IN SPIRIT

The more I uncover.
The more there is to discover.
The more I discover the more I recall.
The more I recall the less I need to stall.

LIMITATIONS

The Truth is there behind all things.
It is there for all to see.
First we must learn to simply be.

We must see beyond our limitations.
Our limitations blind us to all things.
They prevent us from seeing the joy that real truth brings.

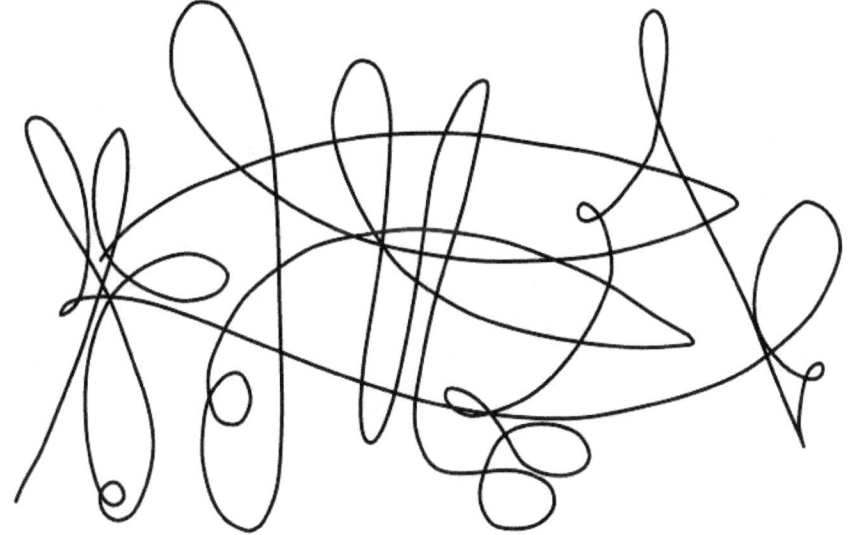

THE DIVINE

Our world of wonders all around.
Miracles and mysteries everywhere abound.
Drawing us ever closer to the vine.
Closer to the truth of All and the Divine.

Ever Present

Truth ever present.
Watching and guiding all things sentient.
It watches and rejoices.
A melody of celestial voices.
As belief awakens.

Dawn Of Awareness

Compared to the consciousness of all.
The world of our senses begins to pall.
All that is and ever can be.
To understand all that is me.
How awesome, inspiring and beyond comprehension.
The truth of this journey towards our ascension.

I Stumble

I stumble and wonder why.
I speak the truth but some say I lie.
I know that in my life I only want what is best.
All this experienced on my way to night's rest.

I constantly help and nurture others.
Even though at times my life it seemingly smothers.
I know we are all one.
From right back from whence begun.

If I hurt others, then it hurts me;
just as damaging distant roots hurt the tree.
Others will finally see;
that humanity wants to be one with all and free.

Emotions And Feelings

Emotions are not to be taken lightly.
Even though they are often seen as fickle and flighty.
They come with Grace that allows us to feel.
Feelings help us decipher the reason for our birth.
Here amongst the trials and joys of this Earth.

Feelings provide us with direction.
They fill us with good and bad sensation.
We can feel and follow them.
They will show us through this convoluted pathway we follow.
These feelings help us find our best way to tomorrow.

Feelings teach love and hate.
Feelings show how to arrive and not be late.
Feelings show our true worth.
Feelings show best how to live upon this Earth.
Feelings are what set Humans apart.
Feelings are what confirm we are on the right path.

Touch

When you touch another;
you find you touch yourself.
When you give to another;
you uncover your true worth.
When your hand finds another's hand;
You find the way to be strong and stand.

THE GENTLE TOUCH

The gentle touch can soothe and caress.
The gentle touch can provide healing and tenderness.
The gentle touch will instil Faith and Trust.
The gentle touch will instil strength and hope.
The gentle touch can supply the peace to let go.
The gentle touch can supply the courage not to let go.

Uplifted

A lightening.
A quickening.
A new beginning.

A peace.
A knowing.
A sense of flowing.

Surrounded by love.
Like a hand in a glove.
A cocoon all around and above.

A feeling of flotation.
My soul in motion.
My world in rotation.

Absence of pain.
Nothing to strive for or gain.
No fortune or fame.

This is it.
Right now as I sit.
My whole Being is lit.

From within the flow comes.
My ego hears and succumbs.
A feeling of bliss that becomes.

Floating in sea.
Weightless and free.
This is it, Just my God and me.

Away from the world of form.
No more trials of this life to mourn.
I feel young and reborn.

As I continue on Life's Way.
I will recall this wonderful day.
Freedom found me and decided to stay.

Sharon Cully – Author

Since 1974 I have worked in the Health Care Industry as a Registered Nurse and then in Government and Non-Government Health Service Management. I was also employed to manage systems (Accreditation and Risk Management) in the Public Sector. I have been an Aged Care Assessor, Aged Care Facility Manager, Teacher and Workplace Assessor. This has provided me with extensive experience in the management of people through all types of life traumas and crises. My experience ranges across many cultures and all age groups. My life has been one of service to others and continues to be.

On a personal level I have lived through many of the same crises that affect those I care for. I have lived through death, grief, bereavement experiences and chronic illness. These experiences have added additional levels of understanding, empathy and insight into the needs of others. Most importantly, combined it has provided me the best training ground to assist others who now experience these issues themselves.

As a child I emigrated from England to Australia with my parents. This taught me about isolation. The difficulties faced by others when removed from their social and family support systems. The traumatic death of my first husband at a very young age caused me to experience an "Out of Body Experience" (OBE) and many other metaphysical/ paranormal events. My second husband taught me a different journey associated with self-understanding, self-worth, social roles, social stigma and the inner strength humans are capable of finding in adversity. The most important lesson learnt is that there is no such word as "can't".

An escape to the country from an urban upbringing saw the development of skills related to survival on the land, farming and self-sufficiency. It also taught the true meaning of severe physical and financial hardship. I have travelled extensively to different areas of our world. I have lived and worked in urban, rural and remote areas. This has taught me to wonder and love our world with all its diversity of environments and people.

Difficult and far reaching personal and professional experiences caused me to search and question the meaning of Life. I reached and searched for God. I searched for the reasons why "bad things happen to good people". I read profusely and the material includes books on philosophy, theology, psychology, astrology, archaeology, quantum healing, reflexology, bio energy fields, healing crystals, and all manner of alternative therapies.

(These are only to name a few). My library is extensive. Some of the services I now provide but are not restricted to are:

Life and Spiritual Journey Coaching.

Reiki and spiritual healing.

Music, art and colour for healing purposes.

Facilitation of spiritual self-development group meetings.

Public speaking at reflective workshops.

I love life but especially I love writing, art, nature and music. This is my second volume of the Where We are Now Series. I invite you to come with me on the next stage of the journey home.

EMMA JARVIS - ARTIST

There have been many experiences I have encountered and endured in my short life. At times it feels as if I have lived many in this one lifetime. I have had the joy of many unexplained health symptoms and discomfort to accompany my days; and this is not how I would have described it once. I experienced the type of ill health that resulted in the complete devolvement from a strong and independent woman to a frail one not only of physical but of mind and emotion; so destroyed that total dependence on another was essential. The type of ill health that saw me curled up crying to GOD for help that the pain and discomfort could no longer be endured.

Feeling disappointed and abandoned by the medical world I went searching for answers elsewhere. I found spirituality, I found more questions and I found myself. This search went on for some 5 years. I was led on a journey of true self-discovery and healing of so many facets; and it was on one of the many paths that this journey directed me to a meditation class in the March of 2011. During a meditation my hand began to tremble and shake and this was the beginning of something very new for me. It was also the beginning of my climb back to health and a new way to help myself, Mother Earth and one day others. Information was coming through my hand in the form of Multidimensional Energy Patterns. It is these patterns which accompany and support the wonderful healing words contained within this book. I hope they bring you as much comfort and strength as I have personally received from them.

www.ingramcontent.com/pod-product-compliance
Lightning Source LLC
Chambersburg PA
CBHW072115290426
44110CB00014B/1918